D0606514

Dolores County Children's Branch
PO Box 578
Dove Creek, CO 81324-0578

Wildfires

HOWARD K. TRAMMEL

Children's Press®
An Imprint of Scholastic Inc.
New York Toronto London Auckland Sydney
Mexico City New Delhi Hong Kong
Danbury, Connecticut

Content Consultant

K. Shafer Smith, Ph.D.
Associate Professor, Center for Atmosphere Ocean Science
Courant Institute of Mathematical Sciences
New York University
New York, NY

Library of Congress Cataloging-in-Publication Data

Trammel, Howard K.
  Wildfires / by Howard K. Trammel.
        p. cm. -- (A true book)
  Includes index.
      ISBN-13: 978-0-531-16887-5 (lib. bdg.)   978-0-531-21355-1 (pbk.)
      ISBN-10: 0-531-16887-5 (lib. bdg.)   0-531-21355-2 (pbk.)

1. Wildfires--Juvenile literature. I. Title. II. Series.

  SD421.23.T73 2009
  634.9'618--dc22   2008014796

Produced by Weldon Owen Education Inc.

©2009 Scholastic Inc.

Find the Truth!

Everything you are about to read is true *except* for one of the sentences on this page.

Which one is **TRUE**?

T or F Every wildfire has to be put out as quickly as possible.

T or F Firefighters often start fires to stop a wildfire.

Find the answers in this book.

Contents

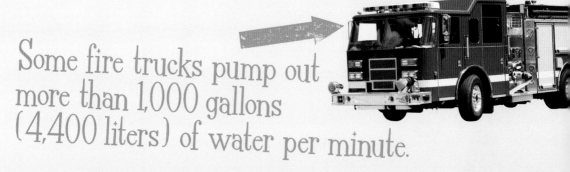

Some fire trucks pump out
more than 1,000 gallons
(4,400 liters) of water per minute.

4

Flowering plants called fireweed grow well in areas burned by wildfires.

THE BIG TRUTH!

Air Attack

5 Wildfires and Nature

Intense heat from a fire lifts smoke high into the air. As the fire cools, the smoke will stay closer to the ground.

CHAPTER 1

Where There's Smoke

You smell smoke in the air. You look around, but it's not coming from a chimney. Besides, it's summer, and it's too hot to make a fire in the fireplace. Miles away, over the wooded hills outside of town, you can see gray smoke reaching far up into the air. It's a wildfire!

← An area of U.S. wildland about the size of Vermont burns every year.

During the 2007 California wildfires, 500,000 people had to leave their homes.

The 2007 California fires forced more people to flee their homes than ever before in California.

The smell of smoke gets stronger. The fire is headed your way! The television news shows firefighters battling the blaze. Soon the television reporter makes an official announcement. People in your area need to **evacuate**!

You and your family quickly gather clothing and some of your most precious possessions. You scoop up your dog. When you return home a week later, everything is gone. The fire is out, but your house has burned to the ground.

In 2007, more than a thousand people in California lost everything they owned to wildfires.

Communities with large forests, such as Big Sur, in California, are often threatened by wildfires.

CHAPTER 2

What Is a Wildfire?

Wildfires are part of the normal life cycle of some forests and grasslands. Many are caused by natural events, such as lightning. Most wildfires burn themselves out before they reach towns or cities. However, a small number of them become very destructive. They may burn too hot, or spread from wildlands to places where people live.

Trees can explode if the water in their wood turns to steam very quickly.

Starting Fires

Wildfires usually start when the weather is hot and dry. When it doesn't rain for a long time, grasses and bushes get very dry. They can catch fire easily, starting what is called a surface fire, or **brush fire**. Although lightning causes many of these fires, others are started by people. Burning trash or campfires can start wildfires. Cigarettes, sparks from machines, and fireworks are other causes.

Parks allow campfires when weather conditions are not too hot and dry. Even in damp weather, there is a forest-fire risk if fires are not properly put out.

The Fire Triangle

Fires need three things to keep burning:

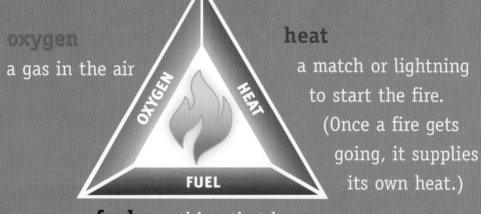

oxygen
a gas in the air

heat
a match or lightning
to start the fire.
(Once a fire gets
going, it supplies
its own heat.)

fuel anything that burns

To put out a fire, firefighters try to take away
at least one of these three things:

fuel   by clearing a strip of land.
heat   by spraying the fuel with water.
            (When water **vaporizes** in the heat of a
            fire, it reduces the temperature around it.)
oxygen   by spraying water.
            (Water vapor crowds out oxygen in the air.)

Types of Fires

A brush fire burns grasses, bushes, and dead branches, but it leaves big trees standing. Clearing out dead leaves and trees can make forests healthier. But if there is too much fuel, the fire will grow too big. The top layer of **foliage** on the trees will start burning. This is called a **crown fire**. It spreads from the top of one tree to the next.

Crown fires are very dangerous to forest creatures. This kind of fire can spread too quickly for animals to escape.

14

If a wildfire gets hot enough and big enough, it turns into a firestorm. Firestorms are so powerful that they make their own weather. They suck in air and create high winds. These winds can carry **embers** more than half a mile ahead of the fire. Smoke from a really large fire can reach thousands of feet into the air. Firestorms can even start tornadoes made of fire, called **fire whirls**.

Fire whirls can be thousands of feet high.

The Yellowstone fire of 1988 was the worst in the park's history.

CHAPTER 3

Famous Fires

Yellowstone National Park is one of the largest parks in the United States. It is larger than the states of Rhode Island and Delaware combined. In June 1988, a few wildfires started in the park. At first, the National Park Service was not concerned. People thought rain would soon put out the fires.

On August 20, 1988, an area in Yellowstone more than six times the size of Manhattan burned.

As fires raged in Yellowstone, lightning started new fires in different parts of the park.

Hot, Dry, and Windy

After five years of very wet summers, the summer of 1988 was the driest on record in Yellowstone. By July, it was clear that the National Park Service needed to put out the fires. More than 9,500 firefighters came from all over the country. Some parachuted in from airplanes. Other planes flew over the park dumping water. The government sent 4,000 soldiers to help. However, the fires continued to spread.

Strong winds made the fires burn hotter and move faster. Soon, firestorms raged all over Yellowstone. Embers blew from the tops of tall trees to start new fires up to 1 mile (1.6 kilometers) away. All summer and into the fall, the firefighting teams battled the flames. Almost half of the huge park burned. The fires were just too big and too powerful to stop.

Firefighters concentrated on saving lives and property. They sprayed foam onto buildings to protect them from fire.

Yellowstone Recovers

In September, rain and snow began to slow the spread of the fires. However, it was only in November, with winter weather, that the fires stopped burning completely. Despite the massive firefighting effort, the fires raged until nature stopped them.

A few months after the fire in Yellowstone, some plants were growing lushly. Ash is good for the soil, and small plants get more sunlight when they are not in the shade of tall trees.

Elk have lived
in the Yellowstone
area for more
than 900 years.

The following spring,
trees and other plants
started growing again.
Most of the animals that
had lived in the park
came back. Twenty years
later, the park was almost
the same as it was before
the terrible 1988 fires.

After the fires, burned pine bark provided good food for elk. Grizzly bears preferred to graze on burned, rather than unburned, ground.

The Oakland Fire

The Yellowstone fire was in an unpopulated part of the country. Three years later, a wildfire started close to a city. In October 1991, some grass on the hills near Oakland, California, caught fire. On the first day, the firefighters thought they had put out the fire, and they went home.

They were wrong. The next day the fire was still burning. It burned shrubs and raced over the hills toward houses. There were very strong winds that week. Embers blew in the wind, starting more fires closer and closer to houses. Soon, thousands of people had to evacuate, as the wildfire turned into a firestorm.

The Oakland fire was fierce enough to jump across freeways.

Four days later, firefighters had finally brought the fire under control. However, 25 people had been killed and more than 3,000 houses had burned. In Yellowstone, everything grew back by itself. In Oakland, it cost more than one billion dollars to rebuild the area.

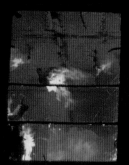

The outline of a carousel horse shows inside a burning building during the Oakland fire.

Firefighting helicopters drop water from buckets onto fires.

CHAPTER 4

Fighting Fires

In towns and cities, fire trucks can race to the scene of a fire. There is usually a fire hydrant nearby to supply plenty of water. In a wildfire, trucks may not be able to get close to the fire. If they can, they have to carry water tanks or pump water from a lake or a river. Firefighters have developed ways of tackling fires that trucks can't handle.

Firefighting helicopters often scoop up buckets of water from lakes and rivers.

Volunteer Firefighters

Countries with large areas of forest often have units of volunteer firefighters. These are people with other jobs who are prepared to **mobilize** within minutes if they are needed to fight a fire. George Washington and Thomas Jefferson are among the millions of Americans who have spent time as volunteer firefighters. Today, the United States has nearly a million volunteer firefighters.

Benjamin Franklin set up the first volunteer firefighting unit in the United States.

Keeping Watch

Every summer, when there is the greatest chance of wildfires, people watch for smoke from lookout towers. Lookout towers are often built on mountaintops. **Satellites** are also used to look for fires.

Many parks and forests also have fire danger signs. These show visitors the danger level for each day, depending on weather and ground conditions.

FIRE DANGER TODAY

Low   Moderate   High   Very High   Extreme

Hotshots to the Rescue

Once a dangerous fire is spotted, firefighters are sent to keep it from spreading. If the fire is hard to reach, **smoke jumpers** might parachute in from airplanes. In the worst wildfires, special teams of

firefighters travel from all over the country to help. These specialists are known as hotshot crews. Many trained, volunteer firefighters also join the battle.

Firefighters protect power lines by spraying nearby trees with water.

Pulaski

A Pulaski is a special tool for making firebreaks. It can be used for both digging and chopping. The Pulaski is named after a heroic firefighter.

Firefighters often make a firebreak to stop a fire from spreading. A firebreak is a wide strip of ground where there is no fuel for the fire to burn. A road or a river can be part of a firebreak. Sometimes a firebreak is made by cutting down and removing trees and bushes. Other firebreaks are made by lighting a **backfire** to burn up fuel before a raging fire can reach it.

Air Attack

Attack from the air can
be an effective way to battle
a wildfire, especially in areas
that can't be reached by road.

Roped In

**Heli-rappellers slide
down ropes from a
helicopter to get to a fire.**

Water Bombers

**Airplanes fill up
their tanks with
water from a
nearby river
or lake and drop
it on the fire.**

Mighty Mix

A special mixture of chemicals is sometimes used to cool the fire, or contain it by protecting unburned areas. It is colored red so pilots can see which areas have been treated.

Skydiver

Smoke jumpers are firefighters who parachute into remote areas to fight wildfires.

Termites often survive a wildfire by staying inside their mounds. The clay mounds are good at blocking heat. If their home gets too hot, the termites can burrow into the cool soil.

CHAPTER 5

Wildfires and Nature

Even though they can be frightening, wildfires are a part of nature. They are part of the **ecology** of many forests and grasslands around the world. Small wildfires clear away fallen branches and excess undergrowth. This removes fuel that could feed a large, destructive fire. The heat from smaller fires helps some trees release their seeds, and the ash fertilizes the soil.

Some lizards crawl inside empty termite mounds to escape a fire.

Most of the time, large animals escape wildfires. They return to the forest after the fire burns out.

Small animals, such as rodents, have burrows deep in the ground where they can wait until a wildfire passes. Larger animals, such as bears and elks, can usually outrun fires.

Plants cannot escape a fire. Many trees and other plants have defenses against fires, however. Some trees, such as sequoias, have thick bark that can protect them from fire. For one kind of tree, the lodgepole pine, fires help new trees grow.

Lodgepole pines have cones that are covered with a sticky substance. This substance stops the cones from burning up. The fire's heat burns away enough of the sticky material for the seeds inside the cone to be released. The seeds then fall on land that has been cleared of other plants by the fire, giving them room to grow.

Less than a year after the 1988 Yellowstone fire, pine seedlings were growing in the burned ground.

A Burning Debate

Wildfires are a part of nature, but they can also be destructive and deadly. What is the best way to control them? The biggest fire in the history of the United States was in 1910, when the Great Idaho Fire killed 85 people and burned up millions of trees. After that fire, the U.S. Forest Service decided to put out every wildfire as soon as possible. This approach caused problems, however.

Firefighting Time Line

6 A.D.

Fire brigades in ancient Rome use water buckets to put out fires. The bucket remains the main firefighting tool for centuries!

1870s

Steam power enables horse-drawn fire engines to pump powerful jets of water.

When few wildfires were allowed to burn, dead leaves and other fuels built up. Trees grew larger and bushes spread. These changes to forests helped to feed enormous fires. Experts argued for change.

By the 1970s, the U.S. Forest Service decided it was better to let some wildfires burn in wild areas, well away from people and property. If no wildfires occurred naturally over a long period, foresters even lit them! These carefully controlled fires are called **prescribed burns**.

1990s

Satellites help to spot wildfires in remote areas, so firefighters can respond more quickly.

1960s

Firefighters start to use helicopters for putting out wildfires.

Not everyone is in favor of prescribed burns. They can help prevent big fires, but they do not always go as planned. In 2000, a prescribed burn in New Mexico got out of control and burned 280 houses.

Today, most experts agree that wildfires in the wilderness should be allowed to burn, and that prescribed burns should be used when necessary. Fires that threaten people's lives or homes are put out right away, however.

Drip torch

A firefighter uses a drip torch to start a prescribed burn at Bear Valley, Oregon. A drip torch drops lighted fuel onto the ground.

The Forest in Your Backyard

As the world's population grows, it becomes more difficult to let wildfires burn. More and more people build their homes in suburbs that border directly on forests or grasslands. In these areas, fires can easily spread from wildlands to people's houses. People who live nearby often want all wildfires put out right away. However, experts want the smaller fires to help prevent major blazes.

People watch as wildfires come dangerously close to a suburb in southern California.

Fires and the Future

The world's climate is changing at a fast rate. Part of this change is a rise in temperatures, called global warming. Global warming has lead to **drought** in some places. Over the past 30 years, the area of the world affected by drought has doubled. A hotter, drier climate means more fires. It also means that fires are bigger and harder to put out.

Wildfires threaten a town in British Columbia, Canada.

Staying Safe

A wildfire is part of a natural process. You can do your part to stay safe, and help keep nature's balance. Here are some basic safety rules:

- Never play with matches.

- Never take burning sticks out of a campfire.

- Don't set off fireworks.

- Advise adults not to park cars on dry grass.

- Before leaving a campfire, have an adult make sure it is out. They should pass a hand over the ground to see if they can still feel heat.

Wildfires are called bush fires in Australia. They are the biggest threat to Australia's frilled lizard.

Wild and Wonderful

It has taken decades to appreciate the role of wildfires in nature. Uncontrolled wildfires can be dangerous. Yet we now know how important frequent fires are for preventing big, destructive fires. We also know how good fires can be for forest regrowth. The more people learn about wildfires, the more chance we have of keeping them down to size. This will protect plants, animals, and humans alike.

Some giant sequoia trees have survived centuries of wildfires.

True Statistics

Average number of wildfires in the United States each year: 100,000

Average area of land in the United States burned by wildfire each year: About 6 million acres (2.4 million hectares)

Highest temperatures wildfires can reach: About 2,000 °F (1,100 °C)

Oldest evidence of wildfires: 350 million years

Average speed at which wildfires move: About 12 mi. (20 km) an hour

Greatest height fire whirls have reached: About 4,000 ft. (1,220 m.)

Did you find the truth?

(F) Every wildfire has to be put out as quickly as possible.

(T) Firefighters often start fires to stop a wildfire.

Resources

Books

Costain, Meredith. *Devouring Flames: The Story of Forest Fires*. Washington, DC: National Geographic Society, 2006.

Hamilton, John. *Wildfires* (Nature's Fury). Edina, MN: Abdo Pub., 2006

Landau, Elaine. *Smokejumpers*. Brookfield, CT: Millbrook Press, 2002.

Morrison, Taylor. *Wildfire*. Boston: Houghton Mifflin, 2006.

Peppas, Lynn. *Wildfire Alert!* (Disaster Alert!). New York: Crabtree Publishing Company, 2004.

Salas, Laura Purdie. *Forest Fires* (Natural Disasters). Mankato, MN: Capstone High-Interest Books, 2002.

Thompson, Luke. *Forest Fires*. New York: Children's Press, 2000.

Trumbauer, Lisa. *Forest Fires*. New York: Franklin Watts, 2005.

Watts, Claire and Trevor Day. *Natural Disasters* (DK Eyewitness Books). New York: DK Children, 2006.

Organizations and Web Sites

Smokey Kids
www.smokeybear.com/kids/
Smokey Bear has been teaching kids about forest fires since 1950. Learn fire safety basics from him.

FEMA for Kids: Wildfires
www.fema.gov/kids/wldfire.htm
Learn safety tips, and read about how fire experts set prescribed burns.

Wildfire Simulator
www.pbs.org/wgbh/nova/fire/simulation.html
Using this interactive wildfire simulator, see how different fuels and weather conditions will affect a wildfire.

Places to Visit

The San Diego Firehouse Museum
1572 Columbia St.
San Diego, CA 92101
(619) 232 3473
http://thesdfirehousemuseum.org/
See firefighting equipment dating back 100 years.

Albright Visitor Center Yellowstone National Park
Grand Loop Rd.
Mammoth Hot Springs, WY
(307) 344 2263
www.nps.gov/yell/planyourvisit/visitorcenters.htm
Learn how wildfires have shaped the forests of Yellowstone.

Important Words

backfire – a fire started purposely to stop an advancing wildfire by creating a burned area in its path

brush fire – a fire burning in shrubs and low-lying plants

crown fire – a wildfire that reaches the top branches of trees and spreads rapidly

drought (DROUT) – a long spell of very dry weather

ecology (ee-KOL-uh-jee) – relationships among living things, and between living things and their environments

embers (EM-burz) – hot, glowing pieces of fuel from a fire

evacuate (i-VAK-yoo-ate) – to leave a place because it may be too dangerous to stay there

fire whirl – a fast-spinning column of fire

foliage (FOH-lee-ij) – leaves

mobilize – to assemble and prepare for action

prescribed burn – the process of burning an area of land under controlled conditions to reduce the risk of larger fires

satellite – any object that orbits a larger object, such as a spacecraft orbiting Earth

smoke jumper – a firefighter who parachutes into a fire area

vaporize – to change from a liquid into a gas

Index

Page numbers in **bold** indicate illustrations

About the Author

Howard K. Trammel is a writer and editor. He writes books for children and adults. He lives in New York City, where there are never any wildfires, but he still learned basic fire safety when he was a Boy Scout.

PHOTOGRAPHS © 2008: FEMA/Andrea Booher (p. 9); Getty Images (p. 10; p. 12; skydiver, p. 31); Hedgehoghouse.com/Auscape (©John Shaw, p. 41; ©Tim Acker, p. 32) ; iStockphoto.com (©Alex Edwards, helicopter, p. 37; ©Clint Scholz, water bomber, p. 30; ©Cristi Matei, satellite, p. 37; ©CSP, p. 24, ©Daniel Bendjy, p. 43; ©fabphoto, back cover; ©Kevin Mayer, p. 3; ©Michael Braun, flowers, p. 5; ©Nancy Nehring, p. 27; ©Nick Schlax, p. 4; ©Oleksandr Buzko, p. 42; Sascha Burkard, plane, p. 31; ©Scott Vickers, p. 39; ©Ziva Kirn, helicopter, p. 5); Photolibrary (p. 16; heli-rappeller, p. 30); Scott Swanson/U.S. Fish & Wildlife Service (p. 38); Stacy Horn (p. 48); StockXpert.com (©pdtnc, bucket, p. 36); Tranz (Corbis, cover; p. 6; p. 8; p. 15; p. 23; Reuters, p. 26; p. 40); U.S. National Park Service (p. 14; pp. 18–21; pp. 28–29; p. 35)

Every effort has been made to trace and acknowledge copyright. Where this attempt has proved unsuccessful, the publishers would be pleased to hear from the photographer or party concerned to rectify any omissions.